0   5/17

MAKE ME THE BEST AT

TRACK AND FIELD

BY KEN STONE

SportsZone

An Imprint of Abdo Publishing
abdopublishing.com

abdopublishing.com

Published by Abdo Publishing, a division of ABDO, PO Box 398166, Minneapolis, Minnesota 55439. Copyright © 2017 by Abdo Consulting Group, Inc. International copyrights reserved in all countries. No part of this book may be reproduced in any form without written permission from the publisher. SportsZone™ is a trademark and logo of Abdo Publishing.

Printed in the United States of America, North Mankato, Minnesota
092016
012017

THIS BOOK CONTAINS
RECYCLED MATERIALS

Cover Photos: Mark Herreid/Shutterstock Images, top left, bottom left; Stefan Schurr/Shutterstock Images, top right; Peter Kim/Shutterstock Images, middle left); Matt Dunham/AP Images, bottom right
Interior Photos: Mark Herreid/Shutterstock Images, 4 (top), 4 (bottom); Peter Kim/Shutterstock Images, 4 (middle); Stefan Schurr/Shutterstock Images, 4–5 (top); Matt Dunham/AP Images, 4–5 (bottom), 39; David J. Phillip/AP Images, 7, 11, 36, 41; Rebecca Blackwell/AP Images, 8; Mark Schiefelbein/AP Images, 13, 23; Ng Han Guan/AP Images, 14; Claude Paris/AP Images, 17; Eric Gay/AP Images, 19; Wong Maye-E/AP Images, 20; Michael Dwyer/AP Images, 25, 26; Kathy Kmonicek/AP Images, 28; Charlie Riedel/AP Images, 31, 34; Rich Pedroncelli/AP Images, 33; Lionel Cironneau/AP Images, 42; Andy Wong/AP Images, 45

Editor: Patrick Donnelly
Series Designer: Nikki Farinella
Content Consultant: Mike Corn, Assistant Director, US Track & Field and Cross Country Coaches Association

Publisher's Cataloging-in-Publication Data

Names: Stone, Ken, author.
Title: Make me the best at track and field / by Ken Stone.
Description: Minneapolis, MN : Abdo Publishing, 2017. | Series: Make me the best athlete | Includes bibliographical references and index.
Identifiers: LCCN 2016945683 | ISBN 9781680784855 (lib. bdg.) | ISBN 9781680798135 (ebook)
Subjects: LCSH: Track and field--Juvenile literature.
Classification: DDC 796.42--dc23
LC record available at http://lccn.loc.gov/2016945683

TABLE OF

CONTENTS

INTRODUCTION 4

SPRINT LIKE
USAIN BOLT 6

RUN LIKE
GENZEBE DIBABA 12

HURDLE LIKE
ARIES MERRITT 18

VAULT LIKE
JENN SUHR 24

LONG JUMP LIKE
BRITTNEY REESE 32

THROW LIKE
REESE HOFFA 40

46
GLOSSARY 47
FOR MORE INFORMATION 48
INDEX/ABOUT THE AUTHOR

INTRODUCTION

More young athletes participate in track and field than any other sport in the United States. Every year approximately 1.5 million boys and girls are runners, jumpers, or throwers—far more than the annual 1 million football players and nearly 1 million basketball players.

Some young athletes will go on to become world champions. The greatest athletes today come from different backgrounds, and their stories are dramatically different, too. Usain Bolt was a wild child, the boy with "too much energy," before he became "Lightning Bolt." Jenn Suhr didn't start pole vaulting until she was almost through college. Aries Merritt suffered a rare medical disorder that nearly ended his hurdling career.

How did these and other champions end up on the path to greatness? Read on to find out what the best of the best have in common and what you can learn from them that could put you on your own road to success.

SPRINT LIKE

USAIN BOLT

Nobody knows who the world's smartest person is. Who is the best artist on the planet? People can debate that, too. But when it comes to sprinting, the answer is clear. Usain Bolt is the world's fastest man.

That unofficial title goes to the winner of the 100-meter dash at the Olympic Games. Bolt won the race at three straight Olympics—2008, 2012, and 2016. Bolt holds the world record of 9.58 seconds for 100 meters. He did that in a 2009 race in Berlin, Germany. He also holds the world record of 19.19 seconds in the 200-meter dash. And he was the final runner, or anchor, of

At the 2004 Olympics in Athens, Greece, Usain was just 17 and the youngest of 54 sprinters in the 200-meter dash.

Usain Bolt crosses the finish line after winning the 100-meter dash at the Rio Olympics in 2016.

Jamaica's 4x100-meter relay team that set a world record of 36.84 seconds in 2012.

Where did such talent come from? Usain St. Leo Bolt was born in 1986 in a small village on the island of Jamaica. Usain was faster than

Bolt claims he ate approximately 1,000 chicken nuggets in 10 days during the 2008 Olympics in Beijing, China. He now eats healthier food.

SPRINT LIKE USAIN BOLT

- Get in the starting blocks. Your stronger kicking foot should be in front. The front block should be two foot steps behind the starting line.

- "On your marks." Get on hands and knees and back your toes into the blocks. One knee should stay touching the ground. Place thumb and fingertips down just behind the line.

- "Set." Lift your hips slightly above your shoulders. Keep your head down, with your eyes looking a few feet ahead of you. Keep your arms straight, with your shoulders directly above your hands.

- Bang! Swing your arms lightning fast from the first step as your front foot pushes off against the block. If your arms are fast, your feet will follow.

Bolt prepares for the start of the 200-meter race at the 2016 Olympics.

greased lightning from an early age. When he was 8 years old, a teacher promised him a box lunch if he won a race. Usain knew the lunch would have jerk chicken, roasted sweet potatoes, rice, and peas. He won that race, and many more since then.

In high school, Usain continued growing to his final height of 6 feet 5 inches (1.96 m). That's very tall for a sprinter. His height meant it took him longer than his rivals to get out of the starting blocks. But he overcame that and began winning world titles at age 15.

WILMA RUDOLPH

Wilma Rudolph was the 20th of 22 children in her family. She had a severe disease called polio when she was a child. Her doctor said she would never walk. But after getting a metal leg brace, Wilma could walk normally by the time she was 12 years old. She became a basketball star and a sprinting legend. At the 1960 Summer Olympics in Rome, Italy, Rudolph became the first American woman to win three gold medals. Like Bolt, she won the 100 and 200 and anchored the winning relay team.

London 2012

DRILL DOWN!

To be the fastest at your school, try these sprinters' exercises.

1. Do push-ups, pull-ups, and sit-ups. Sprinting is a full-body workout, so your arms, back, and stomach muscles have to be strong, too.

2. Sprint up hills. This activity will strengthen both your arms and your legs.

3. Skip down the track. Raise your knees high and stay on your toes.

4. Jump up stairs. In a stadium, keep your feet together while you jump up one stair at a time.

RUN LIKE

GENZEBE DIBABA

Genzebe Dibaba was born to run—or born in the right place to run, at least. Genzebe grew up in Ethiopia, a country in eastern Africa. Her hometown, Bekoji, has fewer than 17,000 people living there. Yet people from Bekoji have won more Olympic gold medals than all of the athletes from India, which has 1.2 billion people.

IIIIIIIII Within 15 days in February 2014, Genzebe set three indoor world records—in the 1,500 m, 3,000 m, and 2-mile (3,200-m) run.

Genzebe has two older sisters who are Olympic medalists and a cousin who won twice at the Games. She was 13 years old in 2004 when her sister Tirunesh won the first of her six Olympic medals. Sister Ejegayehu was the 10,000-meter silver medalist that same year in Athens, Greece.

Genzebe Dibaba represents Ethiopia in international competition.

Tirunesh, born almost six years before Genzebe, was a great cross country runner, too. But when she won her fifth world title in 2008, she was thinking of her sister. An hour earlier, 17-year-old Genzebe had won the under-20 world title. Tirunesh told

RUN LIKE GENZEBE DIBABA

- Stay quiet. Unlike sprinters, who lift their knees high and take powerful, long strides, middle- and long-distance runners conserve energy with short and quick steps. Their feet don't slap on the track.

- Run tall. Keep your torso directly above your hips, with your head up, chest out, and shoulders back. Look ahead, not at your feet, and keep your shoulders low and loose, not high and tight.

- Relax your hands. Run as if you were carrying a potato chip in each hand. With your elbows at a 90-degree angle, swing your arms straight forward and back, not across your chest.

- Mind your pace. The best distance runners know how to conserve energy until the final kick. Don't rush to a big lead, but at the same time, try to avoid trailing the leaders by too much.

Genzebe celebrates after crossing the finish line first in the 1500 at the 2015 world championships.

reporters, "Genzebe is so young and talented. In time, I
expect she'll become even stronger and quicker than me."

Her prediction came true at the shorter middle distances. Genzebe set three indoor world records in 2014. And in 2015, she was named International Association of Athletics Foundation (IAAF) World Athlete of the Year. That year she set an indoor 5,000-meter world record and smashed the outdoor 1,500-meter world best that had stood since 1993.

Genzebe says the 1,500—about 120 yards short of a mile—is her favorite event.

EMIL ZÁTOPEK

Emil Zátopek was known as the "Beast of Prague." The name was a reference to his hometown in Czechoslovakia and the 18 world records he set as a distance runner. Zátopek won three gold medals at the 1952 Olympics in Helsinki, Finland. He won the 5,000- and 10,000-meter races and the marathon. His fame also came from his legendary workouts. Zátopek often ran 400 meters 50 times in the morning and again in the evening. That means on an average day he ran nearly 25 miles total.

DRILL DOWN!

Interval training can help you reach your personal best on race day.

1. On a track, run a lap at your race pace—your best time.

2. Walk or jog for two minutes.

3. Run another lap at your race pace. Repeat up to 10 times.

4. Increase your difficulty by using a ladder system. Run a lap. After a short rest, run two laps. Then three laps. Then go down the ladder to two laps and finish with one lap, trying to run the same speed or go even faster than your first effort.

HURDLE LIKE

ARIES MERRITT

As a high school freshman, Aries Merritt wasn't a great sprinter. But one day a teammate dared him to jump a fence, which he did. His coach was watching and said: "You're going to be a hurdler now." That teammate's dare turned out to be a stroke of good fortune for Merritt.

Merritt likes to play *World of Warcraft*. His main character is Deconasia, a troll shadow priest.

In 2012 Merritt became the first person to win gold in 110-meter hurdles at the US indoor championships, the world indoor championships, the US Olympic Trials, and the Olympic Games in the same year. But he didn't stop there. Nicknamed "The Hurdles Magician," Merritt then pulled off a stunning world record.

Aries Merritt is one of the top hurdlers in US track and field history.

OLYMPIC TEAM TRIALS

Thirty days after winning Olympic gold, Merritt sprinted over 10 42-inch hurdles in 12.80 seconds. His 110-meter time in Brussels, Belgium, beat the previous world record of 12.87 seconds by Cuba's Dayron Robles. Merritt's time was the biggest drop in the world record since 1981.

Merritt is the first American to hold the world record in the high hurdles since Roger Kingdom in 1993.

HURDLE LIKE ARIES MERRITT

- Which leg goes first? Usually it's the one you kick a ball with. But if you have no preference, use the left leg. It's an advantage in the long hurdle races.

- Count steps. If the hurdles are evenly spaced, you'll take the same number of steps between each of them.

- Get a fast start. You'll need a lot of momentum to clear the first hurdle, so sprint out of the blocks.

- Don't slow down. Let your momentum carry you over the hurdles.

Merritt goes airborne in the 110-meter hurdles at the 2015 world championships in China.

The following year, Merritt learned that he had a rare kidney disorder and a serious virus was attacking his body. His performance naturally suffered. But his older sister LaToya Hubbard donated one of her kidneys to him, and Merritt bounced back quickly. By mid-2016 he was back running against the world's best. He missed qualifying for the 2016 Olympics by .01 second, but just being on the track again was a victory for one of the greatest hurdlers in the world.

EDWIN MOSES

In grade school Edwin Moses wore glasses and was a science buff who built volcanoes and dissected frogs. He also grew up to become unbeatable in the 400-meter hurdles. At the 1976 Olympic Games in Montreal, Canada, Moses won the one-lap hurdles in a world-record time of 47.63 seconds. The United States boycotted the 1980 Summer Games in the Soviet Union. Moses came back in 1984 to win his second Olympic title in Los Angeles. Between September 1977 and June 1987, Moses won 122 races in a row.

DRILL DOWN!

Develop muscle memory and strength with a variety of simple drills.

1. Set up five low hurdles in a lane. Step over them, making sure your lead knee comes up first and your hips don't twist.

2. Set a hurdle flush against a fence. Then "attack" the hurdle from a single step away. Lean into and shoot your bent leg over the bar, heel-first into the fence.

3. For the trail leg, set a hurdle a few feet from the fence. With both hands, lean against the fence. Straddle the hurdle and circle your leg up and over, knee first, snapping your foot to the ground.

VAULT LIKE

JENN SUHR

When Jenn Suhr broke her own world indoor record in the pole vault in January 2016, Rick Suhr, her husband and coach, said, "Jenn can threaten a world record anytime, anywhere, and any place. That is the most exciting thing happening in track and field right now."

Suhr once rescued an abandoned fawn and nursed it to health before letting the tiny deer go.

She cleared 16 feet, 6 inches (5.03 m) that day. That height would have been a men's outdoor world record in 1963.

But Jenn had no interest in vaulting when she was growing up. At age six she played softball. At age nine, she took a swing at golf. At Fredonia High School in New York she added soccer and basketball to the list—and

Jenn Suhr is one of the best female pole vaulters in the world.

finally track. Jenn won the state title in the pentathlon as a senior.

In college she starred in basketball and track, setting school records in the hurdles, javelin, and high jump. But she wasn't a pole vaulter until 2004, her junior year, when she met Rick Suhr. He considered the 6-foot-tall Jenn a potential standout pole vaulter. After only six weeks of practice, she took sixth at the small-college nationals. Two years later, Jenn rose to sixth in the world rankings.

In May 2007, Suhr broke Stacy Dragila's American outdoor record with a jump of 15–11 (4.84 m). Two weeks later, she cleared 16 feet (4.88 m) for the first time. The only woman in the world who was better was Russia's Yelena Isinbayeva, the 2004 Olympic champion.

In 2008 Suhr took silver behind Isinbayeva's gold at the Olympics in Beijing, China. But at the 2012 Games in

Suhr clears the bar again.

London, England, Suhr won the gold medal, finishing two spots ahead of her Russian rival.

The pole vaulting world has changed drastically since Jenn

Suhr played basketball at Roberts Wesleyan College in Rochester, New York. She was the school's all-time leading scorer when she graduated in 2004.

VAULT LIKE JENN SUHR

- Poles can be heavy. To make it easier to run, start with the pole in a vertical position. Then gradually let the front tip drop. It's also OK to slide or push the pole down the runway straight into the takeoff box.

- Practice your pole run many times. Put a piece of tape on the runway six steps from takeoff and become confident hitting that mark. You'll go higher if you speed up in the last few steps to the plant.

- Your top hand should be high above your head and over your takeoff toe when the pole hits the box.

- Push against the pole with your lower hand to help the pole bend and stay away from your chest. Your trail leg—the one that leaves the ground last—sweeps up in a whipping action.

- It's a miss if the bar falls or if you or the pole go under the bar.

The approach is one of the many important parts of a pole vaulter's technique.

Suhr started out. In the United States, boys and girls are now allowed to compete when they turn 13. That's the youngest age for the pole vault in the Junior Olympic program. Girls competing in pole vaulting is still a relatively recent development. The first women's Olympic pole vault champion was Dragila at the 2000 Games in Sydney, Australia.

JAVIER SOTOMAYOR

Javier Sotomayor was the world-record holder in the high jump in 1988. But his country, Cuba, boycotted that year's Olympics in Seoul, South Korea. So he couldn't compete for the gold. In 1989 Sotomayor made up for the disappointment by becoming the first man to clear 8 feet (2.44 m). Four years later, he went a quarter-inch higher using the backward-style Fosbury Flop. After missing out at the 1984 and 1988 Olympics, Sotomayor finally achieved his dream in 1992. He won a gold medal at the Olympics in Barcelona, Spain.

DRILL DOWN!

Improve stomach and upper-body strength with these exercises.

1. Do sit-ups, push-ups, and leg raises every day. These exercises are simple, and anyone can do them without special equipment.

2. Mimic the vaulting action by hanging from a rope and swinging your legs up to turn your body upside-down.

3. Hang from a pull-up bar with your legs beneath you. Bend your knees toward your chest. Slowly lower your legs until they're straight. Repeat this action until it's too difficult to continue.

LONG JUMP LIKE
BRITTNEY REESE

The legend of Brittney Reese starts with a Coca-Cola. Reese was on the Gulfport (Mississippi) High School basketball team in 2003 when the track coach came looking for a long jumper. He offered a cold Coke to the player who jumped the farthest. But he wouldn't let Brittney try because she already was a high jumper and 400-meter sprinter for the track team.

"I just begged him and begged him, and he finally let me try it," she said. "The first time I jumped, I got out to 16 or 17 feet and he told me to go and do it again. So I did it again and he said, 'You're going to long jump, and I'm not going to put you in the 400 again.'"

In 2011 Reese bought 100 Thanksgiving turkeys for underprivileged residents of her hometown of Gulfport, Mississippi.

Brittney Reese was a quick study when she began long jumping.

The high school junior won the Coke. Bigger prizes would follow that first win.

Nicknamed "The Beast," Reese has won nine national titles, three world outdoor championships, and the top

Reese can dunk a basketball despite standing only 5 feet 8 inches (1.72m).

LONG JUMP LIKE BRITTNEY REESE

- Know your approach. Use the same number of steps every time. More or fewer steps can lead to mistakes.

- Focus on your last four strides. They should be your fastest. Your second-to-last step should be slightly longer than the rest.

- Launch at top speed. Your foot should be under your hips. The knee of your other leg should rise like a hurdler's.

- Stay balanced in the air. The easiest method is called the hang. In the middle of the jump, you look like you are hanging from a bar, knees together. The other method is the hitch-kick. Move your legs as if you're pedaling a bicycle.

- When you land, reach forward. Don't fall backward, or the mark in the sand will shorten your jump.

Reese gets good air on a jump at the 2016 US Olympic Trials.

honor in her sport—the 2012 Olympic gold medal. A year later, she jumped a personal best of 23 feet, 9.5 inches (7.25 m).

But a hip injury in 2013 led to two difficult years for Reese. She couldn't reach her usual 7-meter mark (just under 23 feet) and she considered retiring.

Instead, the top-ranked women's long jumper in the world from 2009 to 2013 got some help—from a psychologist. It worked. In March 2016 she won her third

MIKE POWELL

Mike Powell's first love was basketball. But he made history in another sport. Nobody thought Bob Beamon's 1968 world record long jump of 29 feet, 2.5 inches (8.90 m) would ever be beaten. But at the 1991 world championships in Tokyo, Japan, Powell did the unthinkable. He shocked the world with an incredible jump of 29 feet, 4.375 inches (8.95 m). He beat Olympic legend Carl Lewis that day. It was Powell's first world title, too. In 1993 and 1994, he won 34 consecutive meets.

Reese demonstrates the importance of falling forward to get the best mark possible on your jump.

world indoor title by leaping 23-8.25 (7.22 m) on her last try.

Less well-known is her other title: Mom. Reese adopted an 8-year-old boy named Alex whose birth mother couldn't take care of him. She also takes care of others thanks to the annual Brittney Reese Scholarships she started in the Gulfport School District. Each year she awards a scholarship to a senior girl and boy to help them cover some of their college expenses.

But Reese, who won a silver medal at the 2016 Rio Olympics, has unfinished business in the long jump pit.

"I really want to at least break the American (outdoor) record and then the world record, and that's about all I have left to do in the sport," she said.

DRILL DOWN!

All jumpers can perfect their technique with back-to-basics drills.

1. Stand at the takeoff board with your feet shoulder-width apart and knees bent.

2. Swing your arms back and thrust them forward as you explode off the board.

3. Land on both feet and thrust your body forward.

4. Repeat a set number of times, then add a three- or five-step approach. Continue to focus on your form as you jump.

THROW LIKE

REESE HOFFA

R eese Hoffa is a small giant. He weighs 315 pounds (143 kg) but he stands only 5-foot-11 (1.80 m). When he was in high school, Reese won the Georgia state championship in the shot put. People didn't know much about him, so he called himself the Unknown Shot Putter. Years later, after becoming a professional, Hoffa wore a Mexican wrestling mask at a meet and threw as the Unknown Shot Putter.

Hoffa can solve the Rubik's Cube puzzle in less than 40 seconds, which makes him a "speedcuber."

"I love to have fun," Hoffa said. "I'm kind of a clown anyway."

He's also a superstar at shoving a 16-pound (7.3-kg) iron ball. He competed in three Olympics and won a

Reese Hoffa shows great balance on a throw at the 2012 Olympics in London.

bronze medal at the 2012 Games. He won four medals at the world championships. Two of them were gold.

In 2014 Hoffa was 36 years old and recovering from a knee injury. He announced that 2016 would be his last year, and he finished his career coming up just short of earning another Olympic bid.

Unlike the high jump, where virtually everyone uses the

Hoffa once said his dream was to throw in a bear suit after being brought to the ring in a cage.

THROW LIKE REESE HOFFA

- Mind your speed of release. The speed is how fast the shot leaves your hand. You need to put your whole body into the release, not just your arm.

- Find the angle. You need to determine the sweet spot between letting it fly too high or too low. Experts generally agree that somewhere between 37 and 42 degrees is the ideal angle.

- Get it up high. The goal is to release it from the highest position. This is the height of the thrower plus arm length, as the ball goes flying at the end of your arm extension.

Hoffa lets it fly in a 2006 meet in Germany.

back-first flop technique, shot putters have several styles to choose from when throwing. The main options are the traditional "glide" and the relatively new "spin." Hoffa preferred the spin.

No matter which style you use, shot putting requires all-around ability and power. Beginners should learn how to lift weights safely and throw medicine balls. Gymnastics exercises can help, too. Handstands, cartwheels, and somersaults develop body control. Bounding, skipping, and hopping help give your legs power.

AL OERTER

Al Oerter isn't the only athlete to win his event at four straight Olympics. Carl Lewis won four in a row in the long jump, too. But Oerter also broke the Olympic discus record in the process of winning each of his gold medals. Oerter won his first gold in 1956 and his final gold in 1968. He retired after the 1968 Olympics, but he returned to competition in 1977. In 1982, at age 45, he was filmed throwing the discus beyond 240 feet (73.15 m). It would have been a world record if he'd done it in a meet.

DRILL DOWN!

This drill can help a beginner perfect the footwork and arm motion needed to throw a discus.

1. Hold a hula-hoop in your throwing hand with your arm extended.

2. Step with your opposite foot and twist your chest, hips, and legs while swinging your arm.

3. Keep your arm about level with your shoulders.

4. Release the hoop at eye level. Repeat for a set number of repetitions.

GLOSSARY

ANCHOR

In track and field, the person running the final leg for a relay team.

APPROACH

In track and field, the steps taken, usually at a jogging or sprinting pace, before leaping.

BOYCOTTED

Refused to purchase a product or take part in an event as a form of protest.

JAVELIN

A light, metal spear that is thrown for distance.

LAUNCH

To get off the ground.

MARATHON

A race 26.2 miles (42.2 km) in distance.

MEDALIST

An athlete who finishes first, second, or third in a track and field event.

MOMENTUM

The force that an object has when it's moving.

PENTATHLON

A combined track-and-field event made up of five separate events.

SPRINT

To run fast for a short distance.

FOR MORE INFORMATION

BOOKS

Johnson, Robin. *Take Off Track and Field*. New York: Crabtree, 2013.

MacKay, Jenny. *Track and Field*. Detroit: Gale Cengage Learning, 2012.

Rosen, Karen. *Great Moments in Olympic Track & Field*. Minneapolis, MN: Abdo Publishing, 2015.

WEBSITES

To learn more about track and field, visit **booklinks.abdopublishing.com**. These links are routinely monitored and updated to provide the most current information available.

PLACE TO VISIT

National Track & Field Hall of Fame

National Track & Field Hall of Fame
216 Fort Washington Ave.
New York, NY 10032
(212) 923-1803
www.usatf.org/Athlete-Bios/Hall-of-Fame/Track---Field.aspx
This museum opened in 2004 in the historic Armory, which houses one of the fastest tracks in the world. Visitors can roam more than 15,000 feet of exhibit space to learn about the rich history of track and field in the United States. The interactive displays teach students the importance of exercise, nutrition, teamwork, and dedication. The hall also features a miniature replica of the New York City Marathon course.

INDEX

Beamon, Bob, 37
Bolt, Usain, 5, 6, 9–10

Dibaba, Ejegayehu, 12
Dibaba, Genzebe, 12, 15–16
Dibaba, Tirunesh, 12, 15–16
Dragila, Stacy, 27, 30

Hoffa, Reese, 40, 43–44
Hubbard, LaToya, 22

Isinbayeva, Yelena, 27, 29

Kingdom, Roger, 21

Lewis, Carl, 37, 44

Merritt, Aries, 5, 18, 21–22
Moses, Edwin, 22

Oerter, Al, 44

Powell, Mike, 37

Reese, Brittney, 32, 35, 37–38
Robles, Dayron, 21
Rudolph, Wilma, 10

Sotomayor, Javier, 30
Suhr, Jenn, 5, 24, 27, 29–30
Suhr, Rick, 24, 27

Zátopek, Emil, 16

ABOUT THE AUTHOR

Ken Stone is a longtime journalist and track writer who began sprinting in fourth grade and still competes on the masters track circuit. His website devoted to adult age-group track and field, Masterstrack.com, won the inaugural Alan Jacobs Blogging Award in 2009 from Track and Field Writers of America. Stone lives near San Diego and is a contributing editor for Times of San Diego, an online news site.